The Inspired Gentleman

Life, Love & Chivalry

Ravenwolf

First Paperback Edition: November 2021

ISBN: 978-1-68489-194-8 (print)
ISBN: 978-1-68489-195-5 (e-book)

Hyperbole Publishing
www.houseofravenwolf.com

Stories of Strength, Love & Inspiration

I Am the Storm

Today is a new day, and you can overcome anything you set out to conquer.

Fate whispers to the wolf, "You cannot withstand the storm ..."

The wolf answers, "I am the storm."

This is your day.

Become the storm.

Vulnerability

He took a deep breath and closed his eyes,
embracing his chance – and his choice –
to finally be himself.
All his life, he'd been told how he should act
and what he should do.
Whether it was older men, friends or even
strangers, everyone always seemed to have an
opinion on what constituted a "real man."
Men weren't supposed to cry – that was a sign
of weakness.
Men weren't supposed to be vulnerable, that
wasn't how tough men acted.
Men weren't supposed to show the world who
they were truly were, lest they be judged.
After a great deal of soul searching, he knew
the only way to be truly happy was to embrace
his fully aware and alive self.
He was miserable trying to fit into the boxes of
what the world said he should be.
No more, he could no longer be what others
thought he should be.
He was through living to please everyone else
… he was finally discovering the path to his
own happiness in the ways that mattered to

him.

He had finally come to that place where he could no longer pretend to be something he wasn't.

A solitary tear trailed down his cheek as he felt his heart begin to beat fervently.

He was taking control of his life, owning who he was, and he didn't care what anyone else thought.

They didn't feel his pain, know his struggles or walk in his shoes.

He didn't live by their leave, and he didn't need anyone's approval of the way he pursued happiness.

Yes, he knew he did all the things that tough guys weren't supposed to do:

He cried at the sappy movies, he expressed his emotions and he wasn't afraid to acknowledge his weaknesses.

The way he saw it, the very thing that the others would say made him weak would make him strongest of all.

He took back his power and, with it, control of his destiny and happiness.

It was then that he knew he could finally become the man he was meant to be all along:

Emotionally aware, strong and free ...
Maybe not in the ways that everyone always
thought a man should be, but in all the truest
sense of the word.
Never again would he let others control how he
thought or change how he acted.
Most of all, he could finally love with all his
heart in the way he had always wanted to ...
Himself, his friends and most of all, whomever
his heart chose.
He smiled at the thought.
This time, it was only up to him,
His choices, his heart, his way ...
And he never looked back.

*This goes out to the amazing men out there
who embrace their feelings, express their
vulnerability and know they're stronger for it ...
No matter what anyone says.
The world needs more men like that –
Alive, aware and strong in the ways that
matter.*

Character comes with a price.

Sacrifice isn't always easy.

When the deeds become dirty,

Class must not sling mud in return.

Those who attempt to bring others down

Do so because exemplary ladies and
gentlemen

Have risen above and succeeded with
courage.

Taking the high road can be expensive indeed
… But the toll you pay to be a better person

Is paltry compared to the price paid by the
malevolent.

Don't sacrifice your honor to revenge offenses.

Walk away from the devil before you're
tempted to sell your soul.

Morality is a choice of character,

And when it's time to play your cards,

It's more powerful to ante up as a gentleman

Than to fold as a scoundrel.

There is no such thing as getting even.

But there is something else far more worthwhile …

It's called getting better.

The Evolution of a Gentleman.

The Best Love

When he met her, he thought he had it all worked out.

He knew where he was going and had everything under control.

Truth is, he didn't even have a clue.

She turned right into left and upside down into right side ups.

She made him want to be a better man –

Not just for her, but for himself as well.

For both of them, for their relationship, for their future.

She changed what he thought would make him happy and what made him smile.

They talk about nothing and laugh about the silliest things.

Conversations about deep feelings and laughter that bubbles up from sheer joy.

She showed him that being the best version of himself is what matters the most –

And what she truly loves about him.

She's his best friend who thinks his jokes are funny.

She's his soul mate who walks beside him in their life.

She's his lover who excites him with each kiss.

She's his daily reminder of how amazing life can truly be.

When he wakes up and sees her pretty face smiling at him, it just makes him realize ...

She made him believe again ...

In magic, in love and in her.

He wouldn't change a thing.

He loves them for all the things they've been, they are and always will be.

Most of all because she'll always be his.

Those Quiet Times When the World Just Melts Away

It's those quiet times,

At the end of our day,

When the rest of the world slowly fades away.

Those are the moments I'll always cherish.

My arms around you, soaking in the events of the day,

Sharing my life with you.

It's not that it's always excitement and thunder,

It's that I get to spend it with you.

Your smile.

Your embrace.

Your love.

Talking intimately with the person I love,

Grasping you in my arms ...

It sets my soul on fire.

I wish I had a magic power in those fleeting instants,

That I could make time stop as I gaze lovingly

Into your eyes,

So that I could love you longer,

Hold you tighter,

And squeeze those beautiful times like a warm blanket that grants such peace.

As we turn the pages of our story, these are the memories that I'll never forget.

The moments that I fell in love with you all over again,

each and every time ...

... when I wished we could live forever

In those frozen moments of love.

They say there will be a moment when you know.

Across a crowded room, you glimpse at her, and all you see midst the crowds of people ... is her.

Your only thought in that instant is that you have never seen anything so beautiful in your life.

Her smile and radiance drown out the world and all you know as your mind races is that you can't imagine spending your life anywhere else but in her arms.

There's no rationale or reason that overcomes you as your heart skips a beat and your breath stops – only the absolute truth that she is the one.

Despite the turmoil that surrounds you and the chaos of life that envelopes you at that split second: that certainty – hers – calms your spirit and fills your heart.

In that moment, you realize that every bad choice and each failed relationship has led you exactly where you needed to be.

You'd gladly kiss all the frogs again and try to make all the glass slippers fit once more that were never meant to … because you had to experience all the wrong answers to understand the right one when it finally found you.

The ifs and questions slowly fade away …

All that you know with complete certainty is that you want to love her for the rest of your life.

Be the Man She Needs, and She Will Be the Woman You Want

Gentleman isn't a word,

it's more than a style,

it's more than a dress code.

It's an attitude,

it's a way of life,

it's a code of conduct.

Gentle on the outside yet savage on the inside.

Take the high road while others choose to make bad choices and live disrespectfully.

Personify the noble gentleman and embody the patient wolf.

Know when to hold her hand and know when to pull her hair.

She doesn't need flowers just on her good days,

she needs a warm embrace and a shoulder to cry on after the bad ones.

Respect.

Honor.

Character.

Passion.

Those are the rare qualities that set a
gentleman apart from an average man.
It's not enough to know the way,
You must walk the path.
A man will tell her she's beautiful,
but a gentleman will make her believe it.
A gentleman will love passionately,
have a compassionate nature and
possess dispassionate judgement.
Gracious in manner and humble in tone,
a gentleman will always ...
open her door, hold her hand, and
know the difference between pride and
insecure jealousy.
Touch her with your words,
pierce her with your eyes and
make love to her with your kiss.
Engage her mind,
enflame her heart and
connect with her soul ...
A fancy watch won't make the time to act
respectfully,
but a gentleman will make the time for his lady.
The clothes do not grant one class,

for a gentleman wears anything with dignity.

Chivalry isn't dead, but it can't be bought, found or borrowed.

It must be learned, practiced and applied.

Manners will open all the doors that even the best pick-up lines won't.

She's a lady, not an object,

So, treat her with courtesy, love her with passion and listen to her respectfully.

Don't make her wait, chase or blush.

Unless, of course, it's behind closed doors.

There's a time for a gentleman ...

And then there's a time for the wolf.

Even the Most Beautiful Have Scratches and Scars

You were broken when I found you,
crumpled midst the emotional wreckage.
Life drained and heart broken, your soul wept
through each and every tear that fell.
But as I took your hand into mine, kissing your
skin with subtle purpose,
The storms in your eyes slowly began to
subside.
You didn't want to believe in love, me or
anyone.
Your spirit was crushed, and your trust gone.
You needed a light midst the darkness that
someone had cast over your soul.
It's always darkest before dawn, I told you,
And the sun always rises.
Wiping away the tears, I smiled past your
anguish into the beauty that hid beyond.
Your reflection doesn't determine your self-
worth, and sometimes,
The most beautiful scars can create the most
wonderful heart.

They tell your journey, weave the amazing story that is so uniquely you.

Scared and wounded, you wanted to trust me, but you'd been burned that way before.

Your walls were high and your heart utterly bruised from all the ones before.

Pushing aside your hair from your tear-soaked cheek, I softly kissed you, smiling warmly.

I can't make the pain go away, and I can't make it all better, but I can promise you to love you, unconditionally.

Sometimes, the hardest part of the journey is believing you're worth the trip.

You can't help what happens to you, but you can decide not to be reduced by it.

I kissed your forehead and stroked your hair lovingly as you weakly mustered a grin.

As our eyes met, souls truly alive for the first time together, I knew I'd forever live in those next moments as I spoke.

Even the brightest stars endure the darkest hours, but when you're meant to become more, you find a way to light up the night sky.

"Baby, it's your time to shine."

And I knew in that moment you were finally ready ... you saw the path, felt the hope.

The look of recognition set in, and I saw the beautiful freedom in your eyes.

I saw more than a look, a moment or a truth.

I saw your soul.

In my eyes, in my arms, in my heart, at last ...

You had come home.

Gentlemen:

There's a time for words, then there's a time for action.

You can tell her in endless ways that you love her, every day,

but there's a time when you have to stop telling and start showing her exactly what she means to you.

No phones, no television or movies.

Just your heart and hers … one on one.

Look into her eyes and feel the rhythm of her soul careen against yours in those moments.

Don't take her for granted and don't be lazy.

Do all the big things … take her to dinner, or even better, prepare a special meal for her.

Mix in the small gestures of love … notes on the mirror, flowers just because and texts that say simply ... "thinking of you."

Give her your complete focus and lose yourself in her arms.

Learn about her hopes, fears and dreams … and share yours.

Don't just be part of her life – share her life.

Uncover everything she is, and you'll find an amazing person just wanting to love and be loved.

Take her hand in yours, hearts in unison and show her the path to forever, together.

It's then that maybe, just maybe, you'll understand that the true beauty of a woman is her heart, mind, body and soul.

Then remind her each and every day, in every way, how very much she is loved.

She Was Beautiful in a Way that Was Uniquely Her

When you find a beautiful wild spirit,

You don't try to catch or tame it.

Truth is, you probably couldn't, even if you wanted to.

Carefree and unique, a woman like her was the rarest of rare, and I very well knew it.

She'd cross your path and make your heart flutter … before vanishing moments later.

She'd love you and leave you breathless, stealing away your heart without the slightest warning.

I saw past her mystical smile and soulful eyes into a mystery that I knew I'd never understand but that wouldn't stop me from diving into all that she was.

Better to have love and lost, they say?

Gazing upon the gorgeous creature before me, I don't know that I could agree with that sentiment.

Strong, vibrant and willful, she redefined the entire concept of "unique."

I was lucky, some would say, to have caught the attention of such a wild thing for such a time, but I don't know that it was luck.

Meant to be comes to mind more than simple fortune.

How can I gaze upon the most amazing woman I've ever seen and let her go?

Truth be told, I can't.

I won't.

I'll walk beside her for as long as I might, make love to her soul and drink in the moments I spend with her.

I'll tango with her spirit and protect her heart every day, in every way.

She's more than a woman, she's a wonderful adventure.

She's wild, she's free and she's a once in a lifetime woman.

I can't define her, and I wouldn't dare try.

The most beautiful people are without definition or predictability ... and that's just part of their charm.

All I can do is try to love her, and maybe, just maybe,

I'll dance with her heart, mind and soul until the last sands of our destiny whisk away unto nothingness.

It's a chance I'm willing to take.

She'll keep me wild ... I'll keep her safe.

A happily ever after, her style, our way.

That's a fairy tale worth living.

Your Love Feels Like Sunshine

When you found me, I thought I knew love.
I believed I understood what love meant,
How it really felt and how it was to go ...
How wrong I was in all those thoughts.

You showed me feelings I had never known,
In ways I'd never imagined,
In truths I couldn't have understood,
When you gave me your heart.

The contentment in your arms,
The fire in your desire,
The love in your eyes
The ferocity of your passion ...
All beautiful parts of you that I'll always
treasure.

Those feelings were just the door creaking
open
To a cascading flood of the wonders of you,
That your heart, your love and your soul

Showed me from the very first time we touched.

You didn't just make me feel loved,
You helped me learn how to love myself,
Held my hand through the struggles,
And wiped away my tears during the pain.

I'll never know how I came to be so blessed when I found you,
Only that I drift off every night and wake each morn,
With a happiness in my soul that you brought to me,
A light in my heart that beats stronger for you.

Come what may, no matter where life leads us,
I'll walk the path with you by my side,
Thankful, hopeful and blissful,
As plainly as the sun's warmth above,
Loving you, for the rest of our lives.

And I Wonder, How Did I Find One So Perfect for Me?

When the still of the night settles around us,
And you're lying quietly on my chest,
I just soak in the beauty of the moment:
Your almost angelic breaths rising and falling,
As you drift off in peaceful slumber,
That's just one more reminder of all the ways
I'm thankful for you,
And simply can't believe that you're mine.
I watch you sleep and whisper all the things
that sometimes escape me when we're
together.
I wish I were better with my feelings and words
sometimes, but I know you see how deeply I
care for you in my eyes, in my actions and how
I love you ...
How very much you mean to me,
How you've changed my life and bettered my
world.
How much you make me feel loved and special
and that every day
Is a joy and an adventure with you by my side.

Your soul found mine and together, we've never looked back.

I try to reminisce to a time before you,

And honestly, all of those thoughts and feelings escape me – almost as if they never even happened.

Truthfully, nothing could ever compare to what we found in each other and the love we share.

You're my true love, my everything and my safe place.

As I brush away the wisps of hair from your peaceful face,

I can't help but radiate a warm smile from my heart.

You found me in a sea of people and made me complete,

Against all odds in a way that could only be fate and destiny.

I didn't really know what love felt like before you showed me, and now I can't imagine a life where I don't wake up beside you every day.

You were the answer to the question I didn't know how to ask,

The hope that I didn't know to dream for,

And the miracle that I couldn't have imagined.

I didn't even know how lost I was until you came knocking on my door,

Pulling on my heartstrings in a way that no one else could.

As I kiss your forehead and let my lips linger,

I realize for the millionth time,

Just how very blessed I am.

I'll love you until the horizon meets the sky at the end of time.

I smile as I slip away into sleep,

Knowing I'll awaken to the best thing that's ever happened to me ... you.

The Smoky Fire of My Rebirth

I know now that I had to fall to my knees to rise from my failures even stronger.

I am not defined by my struggles nor am I limited by what I've done wrong.

No, those times that I fell and didn't know if I could get back up – those were the lessons I couldn't have learned any other way.

I stumbled, I fell, I cried and I hurt ...

But it was in the fires of my pain that I forged the courage to pick myself up and rediscover my power.

There're days when I don't feel like I can make it, when a smile is almost impossible, and I don't know how I'm going to get out of bed ...

But I find a way; I dig deeply and force myself to keep going.

Maybe it's not pretty and perhaps I don't look my best on those days, but I'm okay with that.

I'm always going to be attractive in my own way with as much style and charm that I can muster.

The world thought I was at the end of my rope and that I wouldn't last any longer, and once, they might have been right.

Now, however, I've faced the fires of my failures and emerged a warrior made of the flames that once threatened to tear me apart. I'm not afraid anymore … I've survived the worst that life could throw at me, and I'm still standing.

More than that, I found my voice and my hope. Darkness could never extinguish my light and I'm on my way to being alive in a way that is better than I've ever been.

I'll still have bad days and I'll still get knocked down, but I've realized that I don't have to stay down … I'm more than a survivor.

I'm a fighter.

I'm a believer.

I'm a dreamer.

I have the bravery to fight for my dreams and the belief that I can achieve anything.

Forget all those people who thought I'd never make it and I'd give up.

That's not who I am.

I had to die in the flames to be reborn a passionate Phoenix capable of setting my heart on fire.

Where I've been has made me who I am … I'll never forget my anguish, for that is the fuel that empowers me to push harder and fight stronger.

So, as the smoke settles from the wreckage of my life that was, I stand amongst the ashes of my former self ...

And from the midst of the burning embers of my trials by fire emerges a new me –

Capable of anything I choose, who believes that anything is possible and won't let anything or anyone stop me.

I'm done living day-to-day and minute-to-minute.

This is my chance, and my time is now.

Come what may, I've come alive in a way that electrifies my senses and inflames my soul.

So, bring me the storms and the fury,

I can handle it all.

Some people fear the fire.

I chose to become it.

I've turned my wounds into wisdom and my setbacks into a comeback.

Now it's time to watch me rise and shine ...

Just like the fiery light I am.

I know you're the strongest person I've ever met, but sometimes it's okay to not be tough.

You've spent your entire life fighting – to survive, to make it, even just to be happy.

You're used to doing it all alone and never having the partner and support you've always wanted but never thought you needed … and definitely never got.

I know you don't need me because you're a survivor …

You can withstand any storm and outlast any tough time, of that I have no doubt.

But the thing is, I'm here now.

You don't have to conquer the world all by yourself because you're not alone anymore, and you won't ever be again.

I'm here by choice, and I'll always stand right beside you, your hand in mine, so long as you'll have me.

So, what I'm trying to tell you is that you don't have to be the strong one all the time.

It's okay to let your guard down and let me be strong for both of us.

For you, for us, I can be the toughest fighter and warrior that pushes us through the challenges of life and leads our way each and every day.

You've been hurt, you don't know how to trust someone enough to let your guard down, and I know why.

I get that about you, and I'm willing to be patient as I love and support you and face the battles you fight – because they're my battles now, too.

I'm willing to grow together, with me by your side as we charge ahead.

You're not alone and haven't been from the moment my eyes met yours on that fateful afternoon.

So, come what may, know that I'm here with you, bracing for whatever storms life may throw at us.

Together, there's nothing we can't do,

No dream we can't catch, and there'll never be a day that we don't live to the fullest.

You were once a warrior, survivor and alone.

This is a new day and you're in a new place.

Here, with me, you're more than you ever thought you'd be and I'm happier than I knew possible.

You were a dreamer and lover all along, but you were so consumed with fighting that you forgot how to live outside of the moment.

You're not alone any longer.

We are all the things you've always fought to find …

Finally complete.

Undeniably strong.

Lovingly devoted.

And in my arms, hearts beating together, we will be forever one.

Twice as strong, the future is limitless as we face it side by side.

Let's go set this life on fire,

Starting with tonight …

How do you love a woman?

Completely, utterly and madly.

Tenderly and softly so that she falls in love with your heart … every day.

Loving kisses and gentle patience will draw her closer and caress her spirit.

Connect with her on every level in every way to fully appreciate and begin to understand the diverse complexity of a woman.

Give her passion, intensely woven into the tapestry of your embrace, and set her soul on fire.

Don't treat her like eye candy, love her like soul food.

She'll crave your touch and long for your mercurial connection.

But …

Steal her away behind closed doors and stoke the flames of her desire …

Love her savagely and let loose her true primality …

She'll devour you with consumptive fire and plunge herself into your wild depths.

Lower your walls and open your heart in a raw, visceral and true way – that's what she wants and needs.

Complete and honest love is madness,

But it is the emotional catalyst for our descent into euphoric pleasure that is without equal.

Romance her.

Listen to her.

Embrace her –

Mentally, emotionally and physically.

Most of all, claim her powerfully.

If you do those things ...

She'll never want for anything ...

But a place in your arms, your heart and your life forever.

Gentlemen,

There are truths of which we should all be aware.

Never keep a lady waiting.

Don't disrespect her and expect her to appreciate that sort of treatment.

She's a lady – not an option, a possibility or a choice.

She deserves and wants your full and undivided attention:

Failure to do so will ultimately leave you trying to win her back.

She's not a prize or a possession to be won.

She's a wonderfully graceful and beautifully vibrant soul that can enchant your mind and tickle your senses.

Look her in the eye, hold her hand in the dark and kiss her softly on the lips.

Tell her she's beautiful when she least feels it, Show her she is special when she most needs it.

Umbrellas in the rain and your coat in the cold,

Be the man she needs, and she will be the lady you want.

Surprises don't need a reason or occasion,

Because you love her is the only reason you will ever need ...

And the only reason she wants.

Take her out on the town,

Cuddle her up on the couch ...

But whatever you do, Gentlemen,

Ask to take her hand to dance,

Show her love's last song,

Because you will feel it in her touch, see it in her eyes and

Seal it with a kiss.

Don't make her chase you or compete for your attention.

A real lady won't run after you in heels,

but then,

A real gentleman wouldn't let her.

Dream of Me While I'm Away

There was something so different about him, something she couldn't quite put her finger on.

The way he moved, the way he talked, the way he respected and listened to her …

The way he made her feel like she was the most beautiful and special woman in the world.

No matter the day, regardless of how and why, he could reach across any distance and touch her heart with only a few simple words.

"Good morning, Beautiful" meant something so very different than it ever had before.

"Good night, Love" was always the perfect way to end any night and something she wanted when she couldn't have him instead.

He didn't have to be beside her to be there with her – she had his love tucked away in her heart, always.

He didn't kiss her lips, but her soul.

He didn't touch her skin but melted her heart.

He didn't just love her, he made her feel adored.

He looked at her the way she had always dreamt of, and that's how she knew he was …

The one she had waited a lifetime for.

He was the answer to the question she had been afraid to ask –

Was this meant to be?

Could he really be the one?

She was almost too afraid to ask lest she ruin the perfection of their love.

All it took was his smile, a promise and how he loved her, each and every day ...

Her heart knew even before she did.

He was the man she wanted for always.

He didn't just love her.

He didn't just make her feel special,

He did something no one else had ever done.

He treated her in a way she had never known – with love, respect, passion and understanding.

He completed her, cherished and helped her understand ...

Love is a gift ... a promise she would never forget.

It was a blessing she planned to spend the rest of their lives enjoying by his side ...

Just the way they'd always wanted.

A Gentleman Knows

Guys, the message is clear.

Be a gentleman, even when no one is there.

You can't find character,

you must build it.

Respect isn't demanded,

it's commanded.

Trust isn't given,

it's earned.

And having honor is a choice.

Treat her with respect – every day.

Open her door, carry her umbrella.

Hold out your hand as she ascends the stairs,

Take her coat.

Pull out her chair.

It's not always about the love poems and
diamond rings,

But rather, it's the gestures that come from the
heart that mean the most.

You'll learn that the little things are the big
things after all.

A guy will speak.

A man will explain.

A gentleman will inspire.

Doing more than just saying the right things but also following through.

Be the reason that she forgets her heart was ever broken,

The man who helps her to believe in love again.

Sometimes, she doesn't need you to solve her problems, she just needs you to pull her close and just listen.

Hold her hand, protect her heart and nourish her soul.

Choose to be more while the others decide to be less.

Don't just be a man of words, vow to be a gentleman of action.

Anyone can promise the sun, moon and stars ... But a gentleman will be the one who lassos the stars and brings them home to her.

Be the one who rises above and makes her feel like she's everything, and she'll do the same for you.

If you're the man she needs, then she will be the lady you want.

Don't substitute crass for class,

And don't accept just any woman –
Hold out for the lady of your dreams.
Not a one in a million girl,
But a once in a lifetime lady.
Take your chance to step up
And be the one man ...
Who shows her that true love is real ...
And that fairytales do come true.

As I turned and walked away, I felt the tears welling up in my eyes.

The memories of what we had and the love we once shared flashed through my mind in a long-since gone montage of happiness.

It's easy to remember the good stuff when you're thinking about someone –

My soul couldn't take reliving the heartache and pain that we had endured as a couple.

The bitterness and angst that made me cry so many nights ... I simply didn't want to feel that again.

I looked back over my shoulder one last time at you, seeing you standing there, motionless as I walked away.

I could see your pain, eyes watering, and it hurt me deeply – maybe one of the hardest things I've ever had to do was walk away from you.

It was something that I had to do for us both to find happiness again.

We both knew that we couldn't make us work, no matter how hard we tried or how much we loved.

Sometimes, love just isn't enough.
You travel down a broken road so long with someone that sometimes you forget what you're fighting for anymore.
The love gets replaced by trying to find a middle ground ...
You stop seeing the joy and beauty of your love and just try not to suffocate under the weight of anguish.
And that's never going to be enough for me – and it shouldn't be enough for you, either.
I smiled one last time as I turned a corner and saw you for the last time.
Those powerful moments can be overwhelming, but they're also a lesson of growth ...
Time slows to almost a standstill as your eyes meet for one last time ...
And then, it's like they were never there, such an important part of your life ... vanished.
We weren't ever meant to be and continuing to hold onto a broken relationship was making us both miserable.
In the end, saying goodbye to you and to us was one the hardest things I've ever had to do, but I know it's for the best.

I'll always love and care about you, that will never change.

Some people were meant to be in your heart, not your life.

So, as I close the chapter of our life and love, a solitary tear rolls down my cheek.

I'll never forget what you meant to me and the times we shared.

I'm making the hard decision to walk away to find real and lasting love ...

Most of all, for myself ... I had lost that part of me for so long with you.

Now, I'm taking my power back and forging a new path,

But I'll never forget you and the love we had.

For a time, it was us, it was beautiful and it was love.

That'll always be how I remember it.

Here's to new chapters and happy endings ...

Sometimes, you just have to know when to make new memories and let the old stuff go.

Maybe the next door that opens will be different ... that's all I can hope for.

That, and for you to be happy ...

Such is the way our stories go sometimes.

All my life I've been told what to do, how to look and what I "should be."

They tried to dismiss me, the ones who didn't like the way I walked … talked … carried myself.

If I wasn't like everyone else, then I wasn't acceptable …

You know what?

That's great with me.

Better to be hated for being authentic than to be loved for being fake.

So many wanted to drag me down because I was different from them.

I've loved, I've lost, I've lived – but I did it all on my terms.

So many times, everyone thought I was finished,

That I was at the end of my rope.

They thought my days numbered and

My choices limited because that's what they wanted.

That couldn't have been further from the truth … my truth.

But the thing is, they never really understood me nor wanted to.

Never underestimate someone who has struggled, stumbled and is still smiling.

I'm more than a survivor, and I'm still standing – More than that, I'm thriving.

I'm a fighting spirit that can't be vanquished, a soul that can't be broken.

See, that's the thing about people like me – we don't know how to quit.

I'll always get back up, no matter how many times I fall ...

Stronger, wiser and better.

I live hard and I love harder.

Words can't hurt me, and deception won't fool me.

I've got a full heart and a lot of love to give someone who gets me.

I don't have the time or patience for empty promises or shallow words.

So, if you want to be part of my life – friend, love or otherwise – earn it.

Say what you mean and do what you say.

That's the ethos of who I am, and it's what I deserve ... no, it's what I demand.

Respect, honor, strength, heart – it's ingrained in parts of me that I can't describe.

Save the lukewarm passion and lighthearted courage, that's not what I want in love or life.

So, if you're ready to stand up and stand strong,

I'll be right here, shining brighter than ever,

Waiting to love and respect you.

I've got a big heart and a tougher skin.

I'm a lover.

I'm a fighter.

I'm a dreamer.

Love me or leave me, I'm okay with not being everyone's taste.

But can you accept me, with all my flaws and mistakes, my scars and baggage … without trying to change me?

I love me just the way I am.

The question is … can you?

I Hope You Find a Love That Inspires Dancing

I hope you find the one-of-a-kind love
That fills your heart with joy and
Soothes your soul with absolute peace ...
The embrace that finally feels like home.
I hope you do all the things that make you feel
alive:
Dancing in the kitchen making dinner,
Cuddling on the couch watching the rain,
Falling asleep together on lazy Sunday
afternoons.
I hope you find the kind of amazing love
That leaves you breathless after kisses,
Making countless memories out of the
moments
That will ever warm your heart across your
lifetime.
I hope that together, you chase your dreams,
Face the storms side by side,
Take the trips to seek new adventures and
Create the life and love you've always
deserved.

Most of all, my wish for you is that you find the
person who makes you better than you ever
thought possible …
Who lifts you up and makes you stronger …
Able to walk hand in hand towards forever.
And most of all,
I hope you find the one …
Who inspires you to fall in love with them
Each and every day for the rest of your lives.

Bravery

All his life, they told him he had to be strong.

He was told to repress his feelings and guard who he truly was.

He yearned to release the emotions that he had locked away behind high walls … but they called that weak.

To give into his soul and show the world his truth would be his undoing … or so he thought.

He fought for the courage to be brave … not for the strength to overcome …

To face the feelings overwhelming the walls around his heart … to become who he was meant to be instead of who he was told to be.

He soon learned that the hardest challenge was showing the woman he loved the true depth of his soul.

He lacked the words and often the tenacity to let his feelings pour forth.

He yearned to understand her, to share all of himself with her on a level that scared him.

Only when he was heart-to-heart with her did he begin to understand the true depths of real and meaningful love.

She loved his strength but, more than anything, she embraced his vulnerability.

His ability to convey his hopes, dreams and fears were what she had loved most.

Slowly, he began to reveal more of his soul and the raw emotions that she cherished.

Finally, when he had thrown off his guarded mantle and become what he wanted to be ... that's when he finally understood what it meant to be a strong man.

It was never about being able to withstand the storms or fight back the feelings.

Truly loving himself and sharing his soul was the hardest and most worthwhile battle he'd ever faced.

For his happiness, her love and a dream fulfilled, he faced the fire he once feared would consume him ...

He emerged stronger, wiser and able to love her in the ways she longed for and deserved.

It was in those moments that he discovered his truths ...

They were real, they were raw, and they were always authentic.

And for the rest of his days, he wouldn't have it any other way.

She loved him for who he was, how he loved her and most of all, how he shared himself with her ... completely.

He no longer wanted to be hard or heroic ... more than anything,

He just wanted to be hers.

I'm not always sunshine and rainbows, just the opposite some days.

It's those days when I have thunderstorms and lightning behind my eyes that I'm at my honest truth.

The days when all I want to do is curl up in a corner and cry … but I face the world anyway.

Everyone always wants to share in the happy days, but there are bad times mixed in and always will be.

I fight through the hard days and, somehow, find a way to force a smile for the world.

Give me the people who will stand beside me at my lowest.

Find me the ones who will love and accept me at my worst.

Show me a partner who may not always understand me but will always listen and care.

I know I'm not the easiest person to love nor am I always easy to understand, but I'm loyal to a fault and I'm real to my core.

I speak the truth when others don't, and I hold myself to a standard that doesn't make excuses or settle.

So, if you want to know me for who I really am, don't come looking for me when I'm happy.

Do just the opposite.

Seek me out on the dark days when I'm struggling and fighting for my smile.

I'm a fiercely passionate and a courageous chaos who does more than survive ... I thrive.

I'm not wired to be anything other than real, authentic and passionate, and I can be a splendid mess.

So, love me for who I am and accept me for what I'm not.

Either way, you'll always get the truth and an undying love and loyalty.

I'm fierce, I'm passionate and most of all, I'm a dreamer.

I do more than exist, I'm alive and chasing my dreams with a zealous heart.

You may not always get me, but you'll always get my best,

This I promise you ...

On my worst days and my best, you'll know where you stand and what I need from you.

If you're going to be in my life – friend, partner or confidant – don't be anything other than kind, compassionate and positive ...

Because that's who I am and always will be.

In the end, you may not understand why I'm a beautiful disaster or delightful mystery, only that I'm one of a kind.

The look in my eyes is unmistakable and the fire in my heart undeniable ...

Dig deep into my soul –

You'll finally see in my eyes everything you never knew you wanted ... until I showed you why you did.

Can you get onboard with that?

The Strength of My Soul

My journey has not been easy,
but then, I own every experience along the way
that has made me who I am.
The good, the bad and the ugly have built me
up, broke me down and inflamed my heart like
an ordinary path never could.
I've come to realize that I'm not defined by the
moments that brought me to my knees, but
rather how I rose again after falling.
I know now that I'm always going to make
mistakes, have hard days and endure stormy
times.
But I'll charge into those obstacles and turn
them into opportunities.
My heart is alive with the fire that has forged
my strength through the tough times, and my
soul is full of my rising from the ashes.
I'd rather burn it all down than to fail … I'm not
going out like that.
I was meant for much more than to wallow in
the dark and lament my struggles.
Give me the courage to always embrace the
storms of today.

Give me the passion to feel alive in all that I pursue.

Give me the serenity to understand my journey and the truth of who I am.

I'll never be the baddest, the toughest or the fiercest, but I'll never quit, I'll always be real, and I'm going to embrace all my triumphs and tragedies.

This is my life and my story, and I'm choosing to live each and every day like the blessing that it is.

It takes sadness to understand happiness, failures to comprehend victory and chaos to know peace.

Rain or shine, I'm doing it all by terms in my own way.

I'll never be perfect, and I'm good with that.

I know I'm amazing just the way that I am.

After all,

The strength of my soul was born on the backs of the moments that brought me to my knees.

It was my spirit and soul that gave me the courage to rise again.

And now, it's my wings that will help me fly higher than ever before.

Strong, alive and free.

I can't always promise days without storms,

Or nights without darkness.

But I can promise you won't have to face them
alone,

My hand in yours,

Our hearts beating as one,

My home in your arms,

My love forever in your eyes.

In those moments of weakness,

When the world has gotten you down,

And life has taken its toll,

Take my hand in yours,

Meet my gaze with your eyes,

And hold fast to one truth:

I'll always be there, by your side, to weather
any storm.

You're never alone, my love …

And you never will be again.

Hold my heart in yours,

Ours souls united …

And always know that we can overcome
anything,

Together,
You and I as one ...
Forever.

The wonderful thing about that handsome man across the room?

He was the answer to all the questions she never knew how to ask.

He showed up suddenly, without a warning, and stole away her heart.

She didn't know how or when she had slowly taken down the walls around her heart, but for him … she had.

Truth be told, she couldn't be happier falling in love with the grizzled man who walked softly but had that certain je ne sais quoi.

She couldn't quite put her finger on what it was, but people just gravitated to him ... and she was no exception.

When she fell, and she had, she did so hard.

She'd been burned before, but there was something comforting about this stolid man whose calm demeanor reassured her amidst her worst doubting.

He knew how to read her and did so effortlessly ...

He knew what to say and how to say it, and there were so many times that she was left speechless.

She was normally the logical and elusive one who used rationale and reason to talk her way out of emotions like love and desire.

Nonsense, she thought.

She had no time for the emotional upheaval of love that just didn't make sense ...

Until him.

She wanted to fight it – and she tried with all her might – to no avail.

What amazed her most about this man ... who had found the way to reach her soul as no one before him had ever dreamt ... was in his eyes.

Across the room, she would be curled up with a book and look up to find him watching her and smiling.

He looked at her with a thoughtful gaze, a warm and sensitive way that somehow comforted her.

Because she knew, beyond all else, that he saw her ... truly understood her for who she was.

He looked past her eyes and could calm her mind with nothing more than a solitary glance.

As she smiled, the twinkle in her eye sparked a warm grin in his calm countenance.

They hadn't spoken a word, but in those moments across the room, they had a conversation of the depth that warmed her heart.

That's when she knew.

He was the one who she would love for always, not for what he said, but what never had to be said between them.

Kindred spirits are just that.

Meant to be.

Try as she might, she couldn't deny the truth –

She saw in him the love that she felt and the feelings that she knew were about to explode.

There's a time to fight, a time to run, and then there was what she had found …

A time to believe in something more.

Him. Her.

Love.

She knew that this was a moment she'd remember for the rest of her life …

When she knew that he was her forever.

Rising from the Ashes

Yes, I went down all the wrong roads and made all the bad choices, I ended up in places I never should have been in ways that tore my spirit apart.

Truth be told, I don't know how I got so down and out, nor how I made it out intact and still whole.

At the end of my rope and hating who I'd become, I hit rock bottom.

Everyone counted me out and no one gave me a chance ...

Even I didn't know how to dig myself out of the hole ...

But you know, that's the thing about a spirit that won't give up.

I don't know how to quit, and I'm meant to become more in spite of my rough start.

It was never meant to be the end of my story, I just had to begin a new chapter – one where the Phoenix rises from the ashes.

I pulled myself up, dusted myself off then fought my way back.

I didn't ask for help and no one offered me a hand, but that was what I needed to forge my own courage and build my own strength.

My dreams didn't have an expiration, and I wasn't going to quit on them or myself.

I know I'm a mess sometimes – a bit of a broken soul with glimpses of beauty stashed in between – and I'm good with that.

I made my way, earned my place, and I'm fighting to make my story a success.

I've got a lot of love to give and a passionate fire that can't be quenched.

Sometimes, you realize along the way that you don't set out to be strong and courageous, but when you're left holding the pieces of a life gone wrong, those are the only choices you have left.

It's not that I'll never be handsome, strong and amazing like the stories of heroes and lovers … I can do that and more.

But I'll write my story my way, and that's what matters most of all.

I don't have to set the world on fire, just be on fire for my own life – the kind of flames that make your heart and soul feel totally alive.

I may be beautifully broken and wonderfully imperfect, but I'm still standing.

I'm still strong.

I figured out where I needed to go and what it would take to get there, so I made a choice:

I'm not going looking for a hero, I've decided to become the hero of my own story ...

One small victory at a time ... my way.

Gentlemen:

If you're going to kiss your lady, do more than just press your lips against hers.

A kiss is a meaningful expression of how you feel about her – make it mean something.

Kiss her in such a way that she'll never forget it, each and every time.

Don't rush in and waste one of those special chances to express your love in a kiss.

Pour your heart into those moments when your lips meet, so that she'll crave the next encounter.

Brush her hair out of her face,

Cradle her cheek in your hand,

Look intently into her eyes,

Don't just kiss.

Ignite your souls with passion.

Soft, but forceful,

Gentle, but deeply.

Sweet, but strong.

Do more than just kiss her lips,

Leave her breathless.

Playful bites in between the blissful embrace,
Become the wolf before the hunt.
Show her that she's about to be devoured.
Linger but for a moment, until her eyes flutter to match her heart.
Your lips brush slightly against hers, the deep breath before the plunge.
Use your kiss to say all the things that you've wanted to express – kiss her every time like it's your first … and last.
If you can consume her soul with the passion and desire that you feel for her,
Then she'll be yours forever.
That is when you'll finally understand …
How it feels to be truly alive.
It is in those moments when your lips collide
That you want her heart to hunger for you,
Insatiably, intensely, longingly.
She'll never forget how much she wants, loves and needs you …
You just have to give her the reason.
Be the reason, with your heart, in that kiss, and she'll love you and want you …
Forevermore.

I Miss You in Waves and Tonight I'm Drowning

I was never a person to miss someone.

I valued my independence and celebrated my solitary life ...

Until you showed up and decided to turn my world upside down.

Love doesn't even begin to describe the depth of us, and missing you falls short of saying how much I need you with me.

There aren't adequate words in any language that I can find that will ever convey how I feel about you.

The moment when my lips part from yours and I leave your side, wistful ...

Is the split second I feel incomplete.

You don't cross my mind ...

You never leave it.

Yet, we're never truly apart,

for I carry you with me, tucked away safely in my heart.

No matter how hard my days may be or how life can wear me down,

I know that I have something special waiting for me.

Your arms, your smile, your love.

For even at my weakest, you hear the song in my heart and sing it back to me when I forget the words.

I could write a thousand love stories and countless fairy tales, and yet nothing my pen could weave ...

Would ever compare to what you mean to me.

My best friend, my soulmate, my forever love.

You're my happy place ...

Thank you for being you.

It's changed my life, my heart, my future.

Right now ...

I just need your arms around me.

That's one of the feelings I love the most.

I love being in love with you.

And then, all of the love songs were about you
...

Now, I almost can't remember life before you and how I was ever happy any other way but in your arms.

Some things are just meant to be – you made me understand that from the moment we met
...

And now I can't and won't see my life and my future any other way.

I fell in love with you, and now I know why this is the greatest feeling I've ever experienced.

There's no place that I'd rather be than in your heart.

He's something she's never known –
A safe place for her heart, a harbor midst any
storm that she might face.
He's her rock, her strength, her reason.

She's unlike anyone he's ever met,
She sparkles when she talks,
She shines when she smiles,
Her light infuses brightly into his very soul.

He does more than dance with her demons,
He soothes her deepest fears with his touch.
Her moods and battles just seem to balance
out
When he places his hand in hers.

He didn't know what it meant to not be alone,
Used to standing strong and living solo,
He wasn't used to someone who would be
there,
Supporting him like she does through it all.

He lives in a way that makes her pulse race,
Invigorating her spirit with his fearless attitude,
He brings her to edge of the wild before
Whispering to her soul of love's promise.

She brings a peace to his heart he's never found,
A place of rest that whispers to him in the quiet,
Telling him it's okay to be himself, to be loved,
That he's safe with her, in her arms, forever.

No matter her flights of fancy,
Regardless of where her mind may wander,
When she's settled back to earth,
She knows the solace she found in him, her anchor.

He never knew how to chase his dreams,
Let his hopes and spirit soar with the heavens
Until she showed up and made him realize,
Sometimes you have to find the wings you had all along.

They were a pair unlike any other,
Checks and balances, yin and yang.
They completed each other like a jigsaw
puzzle,
Found each other against impossible odds,
Believing when love seemed so far away,
They discovered the most unlikely thing in an
improbable way.

The perfectly imperfect love of two people
Who never gave up on the dream that
One day, they too,
Would find their happily ever after.
They found that and so much more ...
In each other, now and for always.

You Never Think the Last Time is the Last Time

Tomorrow isn't promised to any of us, so seize the opportunity and live in the moment.

Make the most of the time you've been given – don't let chances to enjoy life and love slip away.

Appreciate those times when your heart is full ... Capture those frozen instants of beautiful feelings and tuck them away in your heart, in your memories.

Don't miss an opportunity to express how you feel or to let them know how special they are.

Tell her that you love her ... every chance you get.

Show him that you care about him, each and every day.

Celebrate more than the milestones and major events – do the little things and enjoy them.

Cook him dinner.

Run her bath and have a glass of wine waiting.

Plan a weekend getaway.

Hold hands during the movie.

Love a little longer, a little harder.

Leave her a love note.

Make him breakfast in bed.

Call in sick to stay home together and snuggle.

Book a hotel room in town for tonight.

Go on a picnic.

Return to where you had your first date.

Take the time, make the chances and seize today.

Show them you love them in countless endless ways ...

Don't let tomorrow come and leave you wishing you'd done more, said more, felt more.

Love with all your heart today ...

Passionately, patiently, unselfishly and deeply ... Live fully in those moments and experience everything you can.

You deserve it, and you'll always remember these small treasure troves of time that warm your hearts.

Fall in love with each other and with being alive ... all over again, every day.

Cherish it.

Enjoy it.

Savor it.

Make the moments into memories and you'll never say, "what if?"

That's the secret to a life well lived.

Love like this is your last chance and live like everything is a miracle.

Today, tomorrow and forever ...

Looking back, you'll be glad you did.

With Each Laugh & Smile

Why am I so madly in love with you?

It's so much more than your beauty or what you say, more than your adorable smirk or the clever quips you make.

I'm at a loss for words to describe the effect you have on me ...

It's in the way you smile,

the twinkle in your eye and even in the way you carry yourself.

Your charm, your personality, your heart and soul ...

There are countless reasons why I'm so enamored with you that I'd like to spend the rest of my days enjoying you.

Truth is, I've decided simply to embrace every day and show you in countless ways the amazing blessing you are to me ...

To appreciate the person you are and everything you mean to me.

When you smiled, you had my attention.

When you talked, you captured my mind.

When you laughed, you stole my heart.

When you looked in my eyes, you won my love forever.

I thought making you laugh would undoubtedly make you fall for me,

but every time I see that mischievous and beautiful smile, I can't help but fall in love with you all over again.

Me and you,

Laughing, loving and living our best life ...

The essence of every dream I've ever had for what real love would truly be.

That's my promise and hope for every tomorrow.

Until then, I'll simply drink in the beautiful hue of your sparkling eyes,

I'll smile at your joyful laughter,

And most of all,

I'll embrace you with every part of my heart, mind and soul.

Just know this:

You'll always find me waiting for you ... on the steps to forever,

Loving you, endlessly.

The Priority

If you want to write a beautiful love story, start with the things that matter most:

Love, respect, passion, honesty.

But that, my friends, just begins your tale.

Falling in love happens every day, all around us ...

Love yourself first and let the love of others follow.

It's wonderful, captivating and will take your breath away.

But if you want a real and lasting relationship, the kind that transcends challenges and hard times,

You must be willing to do what it takes to fall in love ... every single day.

If you want a love story, then take the time to write quality chapters.

Put in the work, be thoughtful and make her a priority.

Communicate your hopes, dreams and desires.

If you want to share a life with someone, then share your heart openly and freely.

They fell in love with you –

Share your heart, mind and soul to remind them why … often.

Don't be afraid to expose your vulnerabilities, for the right person will love you even more for doing so.

Make respect and appreciation priorities for your relationship.

Their time, their needs and their heart should always be valued.

If you want to be treated with respect, then carry yourself with dignity.

Character breeds class.

Don't be lazy in love.

Write her a love note.

Surprise her with ice cream.

Plan a date.

Cook him breakfast in bed.

Have pride …

In yourself, your partner and your relationship.

Make them feel special by being proud of your love.

In the end, choose to have an unforgettable love story.

Every fairytale starts with two hearts that found each other against all odds.

It's up to you to bring your own magic.

I'm here to tell you ...

You're never too old to believe in magic ...

And the most beautiful love will always be just that:

Magical.

Choose to make your story the most magical of all.

Every saint has a past, and every sinner has a future.

Where you've been doesn't define you, just like someone's opinion of you isn't fact.

Moving on is hard.

Not looking back is even harder.

You can't grab new opportunities if you're still holding baggage of the past.

Some people were meant to be in your heart not your life.

Be confident in your decisions and your character.

Choose to look forward, not over your shoulder.

Don't be left at the starting line wishing you'd run the race.

Get out there and don't look back.

It's your life and your story

You can't write a new opening act, but you can start a new chapter.

Make it one that's worth retelling.

A Timeless Recipe

True elegance, sophistication and beauty are timeless.

It's not about a number, it's about character, class and charisma.

Those few who exude irresistibility do so because they are honorable in their actions, humble in their success, and confident in their attitude.

True beauty is the inner light that never dims, never judges and never steps on another to rise above.

That character shines through any darkness and succeeds through any adversity, with humility and honor, and those qualities make them irresistible for a lifetime.

Ego and attitude do not enhance anyone's dapper good looks or elegant sophistication.

The only time you should look down at someone is if you are helping them up.

Do you want to know the secret to being irresistible?

Start with a beautiful soul, mix in some humility and selfless sacrifice, add a dash of confidence

and charm, and finish it off with a sprinkle of
honor and character.

That's the recipe for timeless appeal –

We should all try it. It sounds rather amazing to
me.

Make a choice.

Either decide to be successful or choose to listen to the naysayers.

If people care what you do and attempt to bring you down, don't waste your time slowing down to hear what they say.

Their efforts to bring you down only prove that you're above them.

Don't lower your standards: raise your expectations.

Surround yourself with those who will celebrate your successes, not revel in your failures.

If you stop to throw rocks at every dog that barks at you along the way to the top, you will never get to the pinnacle.

Character is your inherent honor and ethic.

The commentary on your life by others is just noise.

Where you have been doesn't define you … rather, who you choose to become is your ethos.

Choose to be a shining star.

When It's True, It's Unbreakable

In those moments of weakness,
When you doubt your strength,
Just look at your hand.
And remember,
Those places between your fingers
Are where mine fit
… always.
I am always with you,
Through good times or bad.
You're never alone.
For you're in my heart
And will always be.
I can't promise there won't be days without rain
Or times without trouble,
But I can promise
You'll never have to face any of it alone.

There comes a time when you realize that not everyone is going to like you.

Sometimes, they hate you without reason.

Stop and take a deep breath.

You're never going to be everyone's favorite person and trying to please all the others will cause you to never be happy yourself.

You're not a Facebook status,

they don't have to like you.

Be real, be yourself and throw caution to the wind.

It's better to be a whole lotta genuine than a truckload of fake.

Let the people who like you for you stay in your life and walk past the rest.

The world is full of people trying to be something they're not to obtain things they don't need to impress people that don't care or matter.

You've got one life.

There is no dress rehearsal.

Do it your way, with your style and let your voice be heard.

It may not matter to many others, but it matters to those who love you.

If you are going to make ripples,

you might as well create waves.

As the haters get out of the way,

just ride those waves all day ...

Trade in those what ifs for why nots and smile.

You got this.

Today is your chance and your choice to make a stand and become a fighter.

We all get knocked down, but no one is a failure until they choose to stay down.

Get back up.

Fight back and fight for your dreams.

Nothing worth having comes easy.

If it's worth it, you'll do what it takes to make it possible and never give up.

No one will fight for you, and nothing is ever given to you ... it's up to you to earn it.

This day is yours and the possibilities are endless.

It's up to you to realize that you can do it.

Whether it's a relationship, a job, a dream, or a project, today is the next step on your journey.

Make it count.

You're only defeated if you give up.

Dreams don't have deadlines.

They start now.

You Make Me Feel Like the Person that I've Always Wanted to Be

From the moment I met you, it was so much more than just love and romance.

You have a way about you that just makes me … well, want to be the best version of me that I can be.

I won't always make the right decisions and sometimes, I'll make some really big mistakes ... But that's just it – I know that you'll still be waiting for me with open arms.

No judgement, condemnation or disappointment.

Love, acceptance and compassion.

Truth is, I realized long ago that I needed more than an ordinary love.

Three little words that meant so much would only be the start for me,

But until I found you, I didn't know how to describe what I really needed.

You make me want to be the best me that I can be, every day in every way.

I always knew the person I wanted to be, but when you feel like something is missing, it's hard to fully envision who you're meant to become.

Because of you, for you, for me, now I know who and what I was always meant for.

Through your kindness, empathy and selfless care, you showed me what love is supposed to be.

Your belief in me transformed what I thought I knew into what I knew I could become.

So, Darling, for me, "love" doesn't even begin to encompass what you mean to me and how you've changed my life.

I always thought I knew what love was, but now, I realize that I never really did.

To love myself for all my flaws and celebrate my failures along with my victories was a notion that I could never fully grasp before.

You showed me it was okay to be imperfect in my own flawsome way.

So, as you look into my eyes and meet my soul in a place beyond this ...

Know that I love you in ways that I can't always express, for words could never do justice to what we have.

You're my one true thing, my soulmate and my love.

Maybe I can never truly thank you enough for changing my life,

But I can surely love you until the last of my tomorrows ...

Into the dying sunset of time's last breath.

There, our love will always burn eternal.

The Best at Loving You

I'm not a poet or the best lover, though I try to
be a little bit of both at times.

I may not have the fanciest outfits nor perfect
lines, but I always try to treat you with respect.

I may not be the most fashionable person
you've ever met, but I try to look nice for you.

There's a whole lot of things that I'm not the
best at, but I do always try.

And I think it's the things that I am the best at
that truly matter in this life.

I'm the best at loving you.

Not a day will pass that you'll forget how very
special or loved you are.

I don't want you to fall in love with me once and
then stay there.

No, I want you to fall in love with me all over
again, every day.

From the little love notes to the gentle back
rubs, I want you to lose count of the ways that I
show you how special you are to me.

I don't need a holiday to celebrate my love for
you with flowers and candy, there's a reason to
cherish our love every single day.

I want you to know that when you come home to my arms, it's the safest place you've ever known.

When you look into my eyes, you'll find the gaze of one who loves you in ways you've never imagined.

When you feel my breath upon the back of your neck, I want you to feel the chills of the passion that is more powerful than you've ever felt.

I'm a romantic, but I'm not hopeless.

Every day, I hope to wake up next to the most wonderful person I've ever known.

That's a love story that I wouldn't mind writing.

It started with a kiss … and ended with an us.

I couldn't have asked for a happier ending.

'Til I find you in the next life, I'll love you until the horizon meets the sky,

Past the stars nestled amongst the waning moon …

Then I'll love you some more.

Choose carefully the message you want to deliver.

The power of the spoken word is mighty indeed.

Don't let your emotions control your tongue, else you might wreak havoc beyond the hurt.

You might cripple their emotions, but you will also slay your own spirit over time.

Define your character with words of wisdom,

Don't destroy your honor with thoughtless remarks.

Strengthen the bonds of friendship with blessings of warm love and those ties will last past this mortal place.

Build your house upon the foundation of love, and there will be nothing that can ever topple it.

Never settle for less than you deserve.

Someone, somewhere, is dreaming of someone just like you.

Don't let anyone love you in a way that's less than.

The right one will accept your past, support your present and encourage your future.

They will hold your hand through the rainy days and celebrate the sunshine beside you.

It isn't enough that you're their number one, but that you're their only one.

True love doesn't take a number and it doesn't require you to sacrifice your self-respect.

Be strong.

Stand true.

Love with conviction.

Know your worth.

If they are worth having, then they'll know that sometimes, apologizing isn't about right or wrong, but the importance of the relationship.

Character doesn't make excuses,

And don't settle for them.

Happily ever after doesn't take detours.

Make yours happen under your terms,

And accept nothing less than happiness.

You can't always be a hero and

Things may not always go as planned,

But you can always love yourself.

And most of all, never stop believing …

Fairytales do come true.

Starting with you.

Be Original, Be You

I've always been different, and I will tell you why.
I'm not afraid of the truth, and I stand behind it.
I'm not afraid of being honest, raw and
downright brutal with how I choose to speak
my mind.
I'm not afraid to show myself
without a designer label and
I don't label others.
No sugar coating or fake pretense.
I am real ... and that's how I keep it.
I'm not afraid to stand up
for something I believe in or
to face down those who would prey upon
others.
I'm not afraid to show my truth
to a world that says I can't be me,
that says it's not okay to be different.
I say it is more than okay to be unique.
It's amazing to be me, to be you.
I will never be anything less than me,
and if you don't like me or it bothers you,

Step out of my light.

If you only want to hide in the shadows, you can do so alone.

I may not be the best, the most beautiful or perfect, but what you see is what you get.

Don't believe me?

Come dance in the moonlight, and I will show you a new tango.

Shall we?

Like a Boss

Never judge a book by its cover.

In fact, you might want to read more than a couple of chapters before you think you know me.

Am I physically attractive? That really doesn't matter.

What counts is what's on the inside, and that's where I'm most beautiful.

So, don't assume and don't guess.

If you want to know, just ask.

If you want to know me, take the time.

I'm not an infomercial, and I have layers.

Anything worth having is worth the investment of your effort.

Don't underestimate me, either.

I'm gonna roll through like a boss, regardless of what's in my way.

So, step up and be my friend, step aside as I come through or step on board and take a chance with me.

I know who I am.

Do you?

This walk called life is an ever-changing path.

Full of twists and turns, the only thing promised is that it goes on.

Through the good times and the bad, the laughter and the tears, know that you are loved.

Don't pass up any chance to enjoy the little things, for you may discover one day that they were the big things.

So, tell your loved ones they are special, soak in the moments of your life and simply be thankful.

You are gifted another day that someone else may never see, so take off the blinders and start living.

Either get busy living or get busy dying.

In this life, that's all you have.

Make it count.

Live with love and love with passion.

If you can't put your heart into something, or someone, then take yourself out of it.

Don't live with regret always wondering "what if?"

Find that which sets your soul on fire and pursue it … a person, an idea, a dream.
That's the flame you'll find me dancing in. On fire or not at all.

It's easy to follow the many …
Popular opinion can seem powerful.
Simply blending in and losing your voice
Doesn't matter when you're a follower.

But the real power comes from standing apart
And staying strong.
Being true to your own beliefs
Is the essence of being an individual.

No one has the right to judge
With partial facts and veiled truth.
But then again,
Courage isn't easy for everyone.

If you come looking for me,
I'll be walking my own path,
Looking past the subtle and direct
Messages of small minds.

I will stumble and fall,
Mistakes will be made and overcome,

But when the day is done and sun is setting,
I'll be holding out my hand ...

Waiting for you to join me in the light.

A First-Class Version of You

You've got one life to live, and there aren't any do overs.

There is no one better than you at your authentic best, so don't pretend to be anything less.

Life is too short to define yourself by someone else's limits.

Climb outside of the box.

Push the envelope.

Dare to redefine who you are by your standards and no one else's.

Do what makes you happy.

Spend time with the people you enjoy.

Be a first-class version of yourself instead of a second-rate imitation of someone else.

Let your life be a statement about how you live and who you are.

Be bold.

Imagine your world by your terms.

Make waves, not ripples.

Make your voice heard.

Roar with might.

Limits exist only in your mind.

Dare to dream and to push beyond.

It's all up to you …

Even the broken can fly again.

It's time to spread your wings and soar …

Dreams are meant to be chased.

As the day washes away,

Leaving you with only your thoughts as company,

The silence can be overwhelming.

The regrets.

The wishes.

The mistakes.

A myriad of memories flash through your mind, leaving you with all of the questions that may never be answered.

The pain sears your soul like a fresh wound,

Each moment bleeding your spirit with dire intent.

The things you should've said, should've done.

The words you should've left unsaid and unspoken.

The actions you should've taken, the choices you wish you could unmake.

Solitude is an odd bedfellow …

Sometimes comforting and peaceful …

Other times, painful and reverberating.

As you fall to your knees once more asking why,

The answers slip through your fingers like sand.

And you feel that you are left only with the reflection in the mirror and memories of people lost.

Tear drops fall and stain the floor as the light seeps out ever so slowly.

Breathe, let yourself feel it, own it … and then choose you.

It is in these moments that you must remember not to dwell in the anguish.

Live.

Learn.

Evolve.

Love yourself, even in these, the hardest times.

Especially in these hardest times.

And when you can, wipe away the tears and get back up.

It is always darkest before dawn.

Your sun shall rise again.

This I promise you.

A man tries to make his mark,

A gentleman makes an impression.

A man accepts a favor,

A gentleman strives to pay it forward.

A man gives orders,

A gentleman inspires.

A man tries to fit in,

A gentleman breaks the mold.

The differences are many, but the results are
more.

It takes the courage to build the character,

And that makes all the difference ...

Between ordinary and extraordinary.

A man takes the necessary steps,

But a gentleman takes all the extra ones.

Choosing Character

Character is a choice and class is an option.

There are many roads to the top,

The steepest of which doesn't require you to sell your soul.

Don't ask for an easier life.

Ask instead for the courage and strength to conquer a challenging life.

Diamonds are only formed under pressure.

Be a diamond.

Be a warrior.

Be a gentleman.

And most of all, never forget your honor.

Succeed with humility and fail with class.

Life is about the journey, not the destination.

Make your story one worth telling.

I stand here at the edge of tomorrow alone, searching.

I do not know where this road may lead, nor what tomorrow may bring, but only that time changes all.

And I refuse to settle for less than my heart desires.

Love may be an earthquake of proportions I may never fully grasp, but I hold one certainty to be true:

All paths have led me to this moment, and it is at this crossroads that I must transcend the temporary excitement and the tempestuous emotions that my darkened soul seeks.

Come to me broken, so that I may hold you closely, as we pull each other together …

A magnificently contorted dissemination of ragged pieces that mesh so perfectly.

I expect nothing and give everything.

Grazing my fingers across the fabric of time, your soul permeates my inner depths.

Hold my heart in your hands, take my essence into yours, so as the road winds and ages pass, I may forever hold tightly onto your love.

Before you, I was nothing.

Incomplete and bereft.

I stand here at the edge of tomorrow, wondering … do you hear my calls?

Will you come to where I wait?

Or does the path lead back to the nothingness, where I will tread my days alone, without love, without you?

I stand atop the apex of my life scanning the world for a sign.

As the first rays of dawn crest the horizon onto my beating heart, I hold my breath and open my eyes, clutching to hope and daring to believe.

As the moments descend around my captivated soul, I realize for the first time that I am finally free.

Perhaps I will wait for you forever on the edge of eternity, but I do so with the promise of more.

My eyes search the horizon for a sign of your coming as I walk into the misty morning of tomorrow.

Perhaps I am destined to walk alone for the remainder of my days, but I do so with the promise of your love tucked inside my heart.

It is there that I will stay, evermore, perfect in the hope of you.

It's Not About Where We Have Been or Even Where We Are Going

Life's not about the destinations, but the lessons you learn, the sights you see, and the fun you have along the way.

I don't regret where I've been, and I look forward to where I'm headed.

Not because the places were always amazing or the sights to be seen always beautiful ...

Not because I learned valuable lessons or discovered much about myself ...

Not even because I'm better for where I've been or that I'm growing into where I'm headed ...

All of that may be true ...

But what matters most is that I did it all with you by my side.

Dreaming of You

They were right all along when they said
money couldn't buy happiness.

In the throes of night, I wake and feel your
warm body next to me, deep in slumber.

And I smile.

Your dreaming form brings me peace.

Happiness embodied …

I gaze at you knowing that I'll meet you there,
in our dreams.

Because your dreams are my dreams.

And they won't end when we wake up, they will
only get better.

Priceless, though it never cost me a thing …

Kissing you softly on the forehead as you curl
up against me,

I know at last that some dreams are real; some
dreams do indeed come true,

Because all of mine did …

In you.

You Can't Cross My Mind Because You Never Left It

I don't know everywhere you've been.

I'll never know about everyone who has hurt you,

Nor the nights of discontent nor days of unrest.

I can't wipe away every tear you've shed nor share in every heartbreak you've felt.

But I can see the pain in your eyes and hear it in your voice ...

And I can lend you my shoulder, offer you my hand and give you my heart.

For all that which I may never know about you,

There's so much more that I do.

I know the love in your heart that eclipses all pain.

I know the broken road that led you to my arms.

I know the amazing soul and spirit that survived and thrived against all odds –

I know that there's no one else like you ...

So come what may, the twilight's fading light will find me nestled gently in your arms,

Loving you today, tomorrow and forever ...
Like the wonder you truly are and always will be.
My one of a kind, once in a lifetime ...
The one I want to spend the rest of my life loving.

The day he knew that he loved her was amazing.

The moment he realized he wanted her for the rest of his life was heart-stopping …

And those were the times and feelings that he held onto during the tough times.

When things weren't ideal and challenges abound,

He would close his eyes and think back.

He couldn't promise to always be perfect or that he wouldn't ever say or do the wrong thing …

But he did promise to love her enough

To make amends for those mistakes.

A wise man realizes when he has the most wonderful woman in his life to love.

A humble man knows when he needs to remind her why she fell in love with him in the first place.

Maybe the way won't always be clear,

And the answers sometimes hard,

But the devoted love of a woman is

Worth more than all the riches of the world.

Hold her heart when you're in love,

Hold her hand when you're in life,

And most of all,

Hold onto each other when the storms come …

For that is the blessing that is true love.

The Sound of My Name on Your Lips

At the end of the day when the world is
deafening,
When life tries to bring me down,
I yearn to hear the solitary sound that
Makes me feel safe like nothing else can,
The one thing I'll never get enough of ...

The wonderful sound of my name upon your
lips ...
The feelings it evokes,
The emotions that I feel,
And the love you've given to me for always.

When my phone rings and I see your name,
My heart races and my breath quickens,
For I know the beauty that comes next,
The one thing that serenades my soul
endlessly ...
Your voice soothing my fervent soul.

When I first open my eyes, sun shining,
I need only look over at you beside me,

And my heart smiles in countless ways,
I'll hear the one thing I need so much every
day ...
Your voice which comforts me when nothing
else can.

As I take your face into my hands,
Our souls colliding as our lips melt together,
The sound that is unlike anything else
I've ever heard before calms my spirit.

The one thing that does all those things
Is but one and the same:
The sound of my name on your lips,
And how that beautiful whisper of love
Says so much in a single word.

Love forever, loyalty uncompromising,
Passion, desire and happily ever after.
That's just a smattering of the emotions
That the sound of your voice stirs in me,
And for that, I've fallen madly in love
with you ...

For always and forever will I cherish you,
until I find you in the next life once more.
Mate of my soul and lover of my heart,

You've given me much more than you'll
Ever know ...
You, me and forever ...
Beautiful in our eyes.

I may not have always ended up where I
wanted to go,
But I've always arrived exactly where I was
meant to be.
All the broken roads and wishes that didn't
come true nearly broke me sometimes.
I never understood why so many doors closed
and why I faced so many dead ends.
My happily ever afters seemed to always turn
into goodbyes and my heart broke countless
times into heartache.
It's hard to keep hoping when every single
time, your hopes and dreams keep getting
crushed along the way.
I never got what I thought I deserved …
Not because I didn't deserve what I wanted,
but because I was worth so much more.
I started being okay with settling and stopped
reaching for the stars.
Everyone will tell you the same cliches "it'll be
okay" and "it'll work out," but you start
wondering who it really works out for.
Tears welled in my eyes so often as I just
wanted to be happy.

I didn't have the answers – in fact, I didn't even have the questions any more.

I had stopped listening to my heart and started listening to my doubts.

I lost my self-worth and began to believe I wasn't good enough anymore.

Yet, for all the people in my life that surrounded me with love, I was utterly alone.

That's the thing about losing your way – you don't know where to start back.

When you finally understand the irony of life – It takes sadness to appreciate happiness, heartache to understand love … it takes darkness to find your way back to the light.

There's days when I stumble and fall, losing the hope that keeps me going.

It's hard to believe when you have all the reasons to give up.

But this is a new year and a new chance.

My journey will be a tale of triumph, but it will also be a story of failures and mistakes.

I've learned not to be defined by my bad choices, and I discovered a way to never lose hope in myself or my path.

I can't go back and rewrite the old chapters, and truth is, I wouldn't want to if I could.

Those are the times that made me who I am, that forged my fire in the flames of struggle.
I've never met a strong person with an easy past, and I'm no exception.
So, these are the moments that invigorate my soul and fill my spirit ...
The times when I close my eyes, breathe in deeply and reclaim my courage when it falters.
This is the time ...
When I trust in the magic of new beginnings.

If she knew one thing about him, it was that he was not just a strong man,

But perhaps the strongest man she'd ever known.

She saw past the tough exterior and rugged facade … she saw a beautiful and vulnerable soul that longed for expression.

He'd been told all his life that men had to be hard, be tough and that vulnerability was a weakness.

Looking at him lovingly, she took his hand and found his eyes with hers.

Her voice, soft and soothing, was the one thing that could melt his defenses.

"My dearest man, you are the strongest person I've ever met but ... there is another way."

His eyebrows furrowed as he looked at her, perplexed and curious.

She smiled warmly.

"I see you … even the parts you hide from everyone else. I know there's a side of you that longs to be free. A gentler, more vulnerable part of your soul. In fact, that's the part of you that's most beautiful of all."

She could tell he knew her words rang true, but that he'd never had the chance to fully embrace all of himself.

He was known for his strength, his courage and his ability to overcome anything.

But for all his ferocity, he'd never found someone to love him for everything he was … and all that he wanted to be.

Pressing her forehead softly to his, eyes fluttering, she kissed him gently and saw the battle raging in his eyes.

Her voice, barely a whisper, soothed his fiery debate.

"My love, the strongest of us aren't those who live and die by the sword, but those who are able to be the beautiful balance of strong and sensitive.

You don't have to sacrifice anything about who you are to become who you're meant to be … except to realize your happiness is more important than anyone else's perception."

Tears streamed down his face as she wiped them lovingly away with her warmest smile.

She had found a survivor and seen what none of the others ever glimpsed in his soul.

She loved him not just for who he was, but everything she knew he wanted to be.

Unconditionally without judgement, she was his safe place in a harsh world.

He could finally become the man he'd always tucked away, hiding and hopeful that one day, he could embrace who he truly was, instead of what he had always been told he should be.

On that fateful winter day, he discovered the love he'd waited his entire life to find in her.

In all his travels, for all that he had done and seen, she was the one thing he'd never experienced: true love.

There was nothing that would ever compare to what he found in her heart, in her arms.

Home.

He needs no titles …

A man is not truly noble except through actions.

They will attempt to discredit, dishonor and disband his loyalty,

But cowardice has no defense save its feet.

Call him warrior poet,

Call him gentleman scholar,

Call him what you will.

It matters not, for names hold no power in the face of action.

Steadfast and honorable, nothing shall sway his resolve.

Lies, deceit and malevolence hold no power here.

Only light and love are welcome within.

The dawn of a new day is bright,

And he will embrace the promise of tomorrow.

The Inspired Gentleman
Life, Love & Chivalry

Ravenwolf

Find more love, hope and empowerment at
www.houseofravenwolf.com
including Ravenwolf's complete works
and quote merchandise.

Evolution is not a destination;
it is a journey.